Rainbow Sky

flash fiction writings

Richard Ashton

Published by Otter Point of View Communications
OtterViewPoint.ca
October 2021
ISBN: 9781777027469

Copyright © 2021 by Otter Point of View Communications
All rights reserved.

… family, friends, love …

Titles

Woof 1
Spirit Dancer 3
Rejoice 5
Stimulus Response 7
Manage the Silence 9
Patience 11
Attitude 13
Listening 15
Words 17
Willpower 19
Faith 21
Testing 23
Difficult Times 25
Rise Above It All 27
Harmonious Relationships 29
Stress 31
Conflict 33
Meditation 35
Breathe In 37
Be a Light 39
Love 41
Harmony 43
1,2,3 Waltz 45
Spirit 47
Music Dance Freedom 49
Le sous-chef 51
Brothers 53
Tuff a Rock Dragon 55
Surprise 57
Celebrate 59

Bundle of Energy 61
Solving the World's Concerns 63
Forgiveness 65
Individually and Collectively 67
Diversabilities 69
Raw Bean 71
Rainbow Sky... 73
Journeying 75
Riding the Wave of Life 77
At the End of the Rainbow 79
One of Life's Little Pleasures 81

About the Author... 84

Woof

I enjoy swimming, sniffing, running and playing.
You can always count on me
to eagerly participate in a game of fetch.
When you arrive home
I like to be the first one to greet you at the door.
My favourite activity is going on long walks.
I always have my coat on
ready to go.
I will protect you if I sense danger,
especially from people who make me feel uneasy.
I might run back to you for help though
if I encounter a bear or a cougar
on one of our outings.
If you feel sad, hurt or tired,
I will sit with you.
Maybe you will scratch my belly.
I like that.
I'm always happy to see you.
I'm glad we live together in the same pack.

Spirit Dancer

When the music plays
the sound travels
to fill the air.
A musical stairway entices
the dancer's spirit to climb.
As the music inspires,
the spirit dancer dances
ten, fifteen, twenty feet above the crowd.
Effortlessly.
Magically.

The music sustains the freedom.
The dancer and the music are one.

Rejoice

Rejoice for me on the day of my departure
for i have been given the opportunity
to shed my physical body
and all that is no longer needed.
To transition into a realm
where others before me,
welcome me,
guide me
and teach me of this new found place with
its characteristics, laws and beauty.
Rejoice for me upon this day
for where i travel
is magnificent in its splendour.
Grieve for what is but
know that i am well.

Stimulus Response

Internal stimulus,
external stimulus,
both encouraging
a response.
The more we can
create and manage
the gap between
stimulus and response
the more we can
influence our responses.

Manage the Silence

There may be times
between stimulus
and response
when silence
will pressure you
to speak,
or to act.
If you can
manage this silence
by not giving in
to the internal struggle
to fill the void
you will not
be forced
into speaking,
or acting,
out of anxiety.
Try to manage the silence
as opposed to
having the silence
manage you.

Patience

Learn to be patient
in difficult situations,
in times of stress,
anxiety,
excitement,
when the urge to respond,
to act,
to do,
is almost unbearable.
Being patient
in silence
can be most beneficial.

Attitude

Attitude is an expression
of the way we
interact with
the world around us.
How we respond
to the ups and downs,
the inconveniences,
and elations of life.
We know of others
by their attitudes.
Others know of us
by our attitudes to
the world within
and around us.

Listening

Listening,
without interrupting.
Giving full attention
to words,
body language,
eye contact.
Being present
in the moment.
Attentive.
The emptying
of mind,
of emotions.
A sacred space.
An opportunity
to speak
as needed.
To be cared for.
Encouraged.
Actively listening.
Respectfully.

Words

Words can be powerful.
They can be used
for a variety of purposes.
Words,
once spoken,
cannot be taken back.
It is wise
to know this.

Willpower

Willpower is an attribute to master
to better one's potential
for accomplishing,
or maintaining goals.
There are many temptations.
Willpower is the ability to refrain
from giving in to enticements.
Willpower allows us to change
that which we have been doing
over and over again
when we desire different results.
Willpower is strength.

Faith

I have always felt
there was more to me
than what I saw
when I looked in the mirror.
This perception encouraged me
to venture on a spiritual journey.
One of the most significant experiences
I encountered along the way
was that initially I had to have faith
without having results.
Soon my faith proved to be
100% acceptable in its outcomes.
These reoccurring realizations constantly
reinforce and strengthen my belief.

Testing

It is always easier
to live confidently
with one's understandings
of interactions and supports
that are available
when life is calm.
It is more difficult
to be positive and confident
in the partnership and guidance
that exists between realms
when life is in chaos,
when difficulties arise.
Times of uncertainty and turmoil
are the true measures
of one's beliefs.
There is no testing
when all is well.

Difficult Times

There is a saying,
"when you get to the end of your rope,
tie a knot and hold on."
For those who are believers
the saying should be,
"when you get to the end of your rope,
let go."

There may be times throughout life
when it seems difficult to maintain optimism.
You may feel upset, flustered,
or uncertain of the future.

If you want to be, or are, a believer,
times like these are golden opportunities
to put faith into action.

Take a deep breath,
pray and be patient.

Give it up, give it over, let it go.

Rise Above It All

As the phoenix rose from the ashes,
I too shall rise.
I will not be discouraged.
I will choose positive thoughts,
positive actions.
I do not need to make myself suffer
by dwelling in negativity.
I will focus on something different,
something productive.

I will rise above it all.

Harmonious Relationships

Our goal
should be
harmonious relationships.
Loving,
caring,
cooperative,
respectful ...
With this in mind,
be one who
works with
this objective,
this outcome,
this goal,
for relationships
in your life.

Stress

A crisis or a problem
for one person is not necessarily
seen as a crisis or a problem
by another.
We all have different
tolerances for stress.
Just because an issue
does not appear
to warrant being
a big problem
or crisis to one person
doesn't mean that
it isn't a significant
worry or crisis to another.
We all have our stresses.
We all have our issues
to deal with.
Who's to say which ones
are more real,
more significant?

Conflict

Conflict can arise
from time to time
from real or imagined
situations,
assumptions,
activities,
decisions,
communications.
Try to deal
with conflict
in an honest,
respectful,
calm manner.
There may be occasions
when conflict
cannot be resolved
immediately.
Times like these require
understanding and patience.

Meditation

Meditation can be the beginning
and ending of prayer
or a practice unto itself.
The awareness of the breath,
the in-breath and the out-breath,
plus the silent repeating
of a mantra, a sound,
a word or a collection of words
to coincide with the in-breath
and the out-breath.
There are many suggestions for mantras.
Choose one on your own
or have one chosen for you.
For meditative prayer choose
a mantra of significance.
One to believe in.
One to trust.
One to incorporate
into your life.
In-breath, out-breath.
Meditate anytime
to focus your being
on peace.

Breathe In

Breathe in
rejuvenation,
health,
strength,
beauty,
confidence,
patience,
courage,
love ...
Breathe in
positive attributes.
Absorb them
into your life.

Be a Light

Be a Light,
vibrant,
healthy,
loving,
alive …
Follow a path
of kindness,
of gentleness,
of love.
Be a contributor
to the goodness
of humanity.
Enhance the web of life.
Be humble.
Do your best
at any given moment.

Love

From the moment Your love entered my heart,
my life has been blessed.
Your love and companionship is a miracle.
Wherever I go You are with me.
I trust in Your love for me.
Time and time again You have shown
how much You care for me,
how fortunate I am to love You.

Thank you for loving me.
Thank you for caring for me.
Thank you for allowing me to love You.

Thank you …

Harmony

Ever changing world
ever changing opportunities
not yet realized.
Believing in more than
the physical senses perceive.
Assistance is available
if requested.
Patience in understanding
change is natural.
An opportunity to learn.
Knowing that when
change occurs it is right
according to the law
of partnership that exists
between two realms
working together
in complete harmony.

1,2,3 Waltz

one, two, three
one, two, three
one, two, three
weeeeeee!

dance with me
play with me
sing with me
beeeeeee!

musical
colourful
natural
seeeeeee!

harmony
beautiful
fortunate
meeeeee!

Spirit

thy Spirit exists
in my mind's eye I know thee
You are all I need

understanding not
thus searching all for knowledge
by Grace I am saved

Music Dance Freedom

welcoming wonders
wise Wind wrestles wayward wants
water washes well

bursting blue blossoms
collaborating colours
speak springtime success

ripe round raspberries
entice ego engagement
sparkling senses shine

beauty brilliance
time flows as the rose plant grows
music dance freedom

Le sous-chef

(I am the sous-chef)
gardener for Your display
of nature's beauty

Brothers

in a caring world
brothers together have fun
both loving each other

Tuff a Rock Dragon

Tuff is a young playful rock dragon
looking for fun and adventure.
Tuff's rock dragon spirit loves the water.

Tuff's best friends are
Sky, a water dragon and
Gus, a labrador retriever.

Gus carries big sticks.

Tuff soon finds the first adventure.
Follow me this way Tuff, said Sky.

We need to travel
over the rainbow to find Gus.

Gus likes rainbows and
playing with the two dragons
in the land of reflections.

Happy first adventure Tuff.

Surprise

The squeals,
laughter,
jumping,
hugs,
love …

So much love!

To have been blessed
with being included
amongst their energy
without them really
even knowing,
or caring,
of my presence.

What a highlight
of this day so far!

Thank you.

Celebrate

Remember to take time
to celebrate successes
that easily become
forgotten in your adventures.

Acknowledge, celebrate, move on.

You did it!
Well done!

Bundle of Energy

the attraction
of a baby`s love

the exuberance of
a puppy's welcome

it is easy to see that
life is a bundle of energy

Solving the World's Concerns

What better place
than outside at
the picnic tables
behind the café
to solve the world's concerns.

Conversations,
discussions,
sharing.

By the end of it all
the world seems a better place.

At least to all who were there!

See you tomorrow.

Forgiveness

forgiving others is a gift
to give to yourself
to be able to release
the disruptive energy
that you have been
harbouring within

Individually and Collectively

co-existing together in harmony
trying to understand signals
of verification to continue

no-one knows what goes on
inside your head
unless you tell them

individually and
collectively we can
unite in Spirit

Diversabilities

Emerging from the community,
individuals with voices.
We all have our gifts,
our shortcomings, our abilities.

We are all different
from each other.
We live and grow
together in society.

We are individuals
with diversabilities
living our daily lives
as best we can.

Raw Bean

I am as a raw bean
welcomed into a simmering
writer's collective stew.

The hotpot has many ingredients,
novelists, poets, playwrights …
potatoes, carrots, beans …

Slowly over time the raw bean
will absorb creative flavours
to be a raw bean no more.

Rainbow Sky

As an amateur
clown magician
strolling around festivals
in full costume,
unconditional love
can be sensed
from those who
appreciate the performance!

A character is introduced.
The clown magician
has something to offer.
Juggling, balloon animals,
magic tricks …
An entertainer to enjoy,
to interact with,
to love for a brief moment.

Journeying

We are eternal beings.

A process exists to create life.
Female and male.
Babies.
New life created.

A life to live.
Journeying and evolving
in wherever,
or whatever
manifestation we find ourselves
in at the moment.

Journeying as individuals
within a perpetual
evolution of creation.

Riding the Wave of Life

the tide comes in
the tide goes out
transcends the thought
what's life about

sunlight sustains
seasons repeat
life's in progress
all so complete

instinct intact
to let it go
to give it up
to trust the flow

evolving life
enlightening mind
together growing
in humankind

the wave of life
for all to save
in our mind's eye
to ride the wave

At the End of the Rainbow

A rainbow is created
when sunlight shines through raindrops.
I was at a place
where the rain was falling
while the sun was shining.
Someone far away
could see a rainbow in the sky.

I was at the end of the rainbow!

I looked around me for the treasure.
I could not see it.
Abruptly I realized
that the treasure
was not around me
it was within me
to be taken wherever I go.

One of Life's Little Pleasures

Coupons are fun!
Today, as I write this verse,
I sit with a bagel and a hot chocolate
both received free of charge with coupons.
The new stores are promoting their businesses
so they have printed and distributed coupons;
the bagel shop, for a free bagel of my choice,
the coffee shop, for a free hot drink.
The atmosphere in the café is pleasant.
The people, the sights, the sounds, the smells
are all contributing
to make this portion of the day special.
The bagel tastes scrumptious,
the hot chocolate exquisite.
And all for free.
What a deal!

About the Author

Richard Ashton is a Greater Victoria Public Library featured author for his publication "Otter ViewPoint" © 2019.

Children's entertainer, husband, father, grandfather, labrador retriever companion and executive director roles have shaped Richard's writings as has a compelling desire to connect with and be led by the Spirit.

This book is an invitation to get closer to the Spirit within you.

Publications by
Otter Point of View Communications
Otter Point, BC, Canada

"Otter ViewPoint" book © 2019
"Otter ViewPoint.pdf" e-book © 2019
"Woof" video © 2020
"Rainbow Sky" book © 2021

Thank you to my editors.

CPSIA information can be obtained
at www.ICGtesting.com
Printed in the USA
LVHW081547211021
700870LV00019B/336